Dangerous Adventure!

Lindbergh's Famous Flight

by RUTH BELOV GROSS

Pictures by SUSANNE SUBA

WALKER AND COMPANY

New York

With all my love to Willy

The author acknowledges with warm thanks the help
of staff members of the Minnesota Historical Society
and the National Air and Space Museum, Smithsonian
Institution; George C. Dade, President of the
Long Island Early Fliers Club; and Elbert Kruger
and Norman Duncan of Fairchild Republic Company.

Text copyright © 1977 by Ruth Belov Gross.   Illustrations copyright © 1977 by Susanne Suba.   All rights reserved.

This edition was published in the United States in 1977 by the Walker Publishing Company, Inc.,
by arrangement with Scholastic Book Services, a division of Scholastic Magazines, Inc.
Published simultaneously in Canada by Fitzhenry & Whiteside, Limited, Toronto.

Library of Congress Catalog Card Number 77-79269; ISBN 0-8027-6309-1, Trade; ISBN 0-8027-6310-3, Reinforced

Printed in the United States of America

This is a true story about a real person.
His name was Charles Augustus Lindbergh.

When Charles Lindbergh was 25 years old,
he did something that no one had ever done before.
He climbed into his small airplane,
and then he flew all the way
from New York City to Paris, France,
without stopping.

It was a dangerous adventure.

Charles Lindbergh grew up on a farm in Minnesota.

One of the things he loved best was to lie in the tall grass and look up at the sky.

Charles wished he had wings. "How wonderful it would be to fly," Charles thought.

5

When Charles was ten, his mother took him to an air show. Charles had never seen an airplane before.

Most people had never seen an airplane. Airplanes were something new.

The first airplanes couldn't fly very fast. They couldn't go very far or very high. And they were only big enough for one or two people. The propeller was in back. The pilot sat outside, in the front.

Mrs. Lindbergh told Charles that airplanes were dangerous. She didn't want him to go up in an airplane — ever. Suppose the engine stopped, she said. Suppose a wing fell off. He could be killed!

7

But Charles kept thinking about flying. He
imagined he had wings and could fly through the
air — over fences, over the tops of trees, over
the roof of his house.

Eleven years later, Charles Lindbergh had his own plane and was really flying. He was 21 years old.

Airplanes were still new and strange to most people.

When a plane flew over a house or a barn, everybody would run outside to look at it.

When a plane landed in a cow field, the farmers would come right up close — and so would the cows.

Pilots earned money by taking people up for rides in their planes. A pilot would stay in one town for a few days, sell as many rides as he could, and then go on to another town.

That was called *barnstorming*.

At first, Charles barnstormed with another pilot. Just before they landed in a new town, Charles would walk out on the wing of the plane — while it was still flying!

Sometimes he jumped off the wing with a parachute.

The pilot got more customers when Charles did tricks like this. Soon the newspapers were writing about Charles. They called him Daredevil Lindbergh.

His friends, though, called him Slim.

Later, Slim barnstormed by himself. He did all kinds of tricks with his plane — spins and loops and rolls.

Barnstorming was a good way to earn money in the summer. But nobody wanted to pay for a plane ride when it was cold and snowy.

Lindbergh needed a job he could do all year round.

When he was 24 years old, he got a job flying bags of mail from one city to another.

It was easy to fly the mail in the daytime. At night, though, flying could be dangerous. Pilots couldn't always see where they were going — or where they were landing.

On two different nights, Lindbergh had to jump out of his plane with a parachute. Once he landed in a cornfield. Once he landed on top of a barbed-wire fence.

Both times, the planes were wrecked. But the bags of mail were still in good shape. Lindbergh got the mail out of the wreckage and sent it on by train.

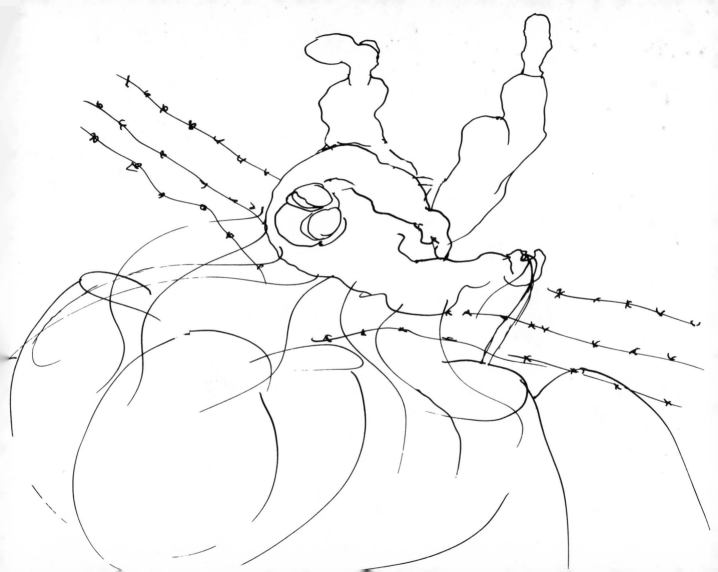

One night in September, 1926, Lindbergh was flying the mail from St. Louis, Missouri, to Chicago, Illinois. It was a beautiful, clear night. Lindbergh wished he could keep on flying and never stop.

What would he need to keep on flying for a really long time? The plane he was flying now couldn't go more than three or four hours without running out of gas.

He'd need a plane with gas tanks that could hold a lot of gas. And he'd need a much better engine — an engine that could keep going for hours and hours.

If he had the right kind of plane, he could fly all night — or longer. He could even fly from New York City to Paris, France!

Paris was on the other side of the Atlantic Ocean — about 3600 miles from New York. When Lindbergh carried the mail, he only had to fly 285 miles.

Lindbergh had heard about a prize, $25,000, for the first person who could fly between New York and Paris without stopping. He could be that person. Why not?

He would fly alone. It might take him from one morning to the next night. But he could stay awake that long.

By the time Lindbergh landed in Chicago, he had made up his mind. He would try for the prize.

First he had to get a plane.

Lindbergh had $2000 saved up — but he couldn't buy a plane for $2000.

He was living in St. Louis then. Some business men in St. Louis knew what a good pilot Lindbergh was. The men wanted him to be the first person to fly nonstop from New York to Paris.

So they got together and said they would give Lindbergh the rest of the money for the plane.

Lindbergh knew just what kind of plane he wanted — a monoplane with one engine.

But the people who made airplanes would not sell him that kind of plane. They did not think he could get to Paris alive.

"What?" they said. "You want to fly alone? In a plane with only one engine?"

The plane would crash, they said. Then everybody would think their planes were no good.

Charles Lindbergh had to find a plane soon. It was wintertime now, and he knew that some other pilots were making plans to fly to Paris in the spring. He wanted to get there before they did.

The others already had their planes — big, heavy planes that could hold as many as four people.

At the end of February, Lindbergh took a train to California. He was hoping that a small company there would agree to make a plane for him. And they did. They said they would make exactly the kind of plane Lindbergh wanted.

Every single day for two months, Lindbergh and the people at the plane company worked on the plane. Sometimes they worked all night.

By the end of April, the plane was finished. It was a shiny silver plane, the most beautiful plane Lindbergh had ever seen.

Lindbergh gave his plane a name — *Spirit of St. Louis*. That was his way of thanking the men in St. Louis who had paid for the plane.

23

Now Lindbergh really had to hurry. At least three other planes were almost ready to fly across the Atlantic.

What if one of those planes started out before he could even get to New York?

Lindbergh left California on May 10, 1927. First he flew the *Spirit of St. Louis* to St. Louis. He made the overnight trip in 14 hours and 25 minutes — and set a record.

The next morning, May 12, he took off from St. Louis. He landed in New York, at Curtiss Field, 7 hours and 20 minutes later. Another record!

Newspaper reporters and photographers were waiting for Lindbergh when he landed.

Soon everybody was talking about him.

The newspapers called him the Flying Fool. He hated the name. And he didn't like the crowds that followed him around wherever he went.

He wished he could be alone in his plane, flying over the Atlantic Ocean.

But there was more work to be done on the plane. And the weather was bad — rain in New York and storms over the ocean.

By May 19th, Lindbergh had been at the air field for a week. He was fed up.

Lindbergh's friends tried to make him feel better. "Let's go to a play," one of them said.

But they never got to the play.

On the way, they called the Weather Bureau. Good news! There was a sudden change in the weather. Maybe Lindbergh could leave in the morning!

Lindbergh rushed back to the air field. He knew that two other planes would be getting ready to take off for Paris.

But the air field was quiet.

What were the other pilots waiting for? Good weather all the way to Paris?

Lindbergh wasn't going to wait. He would start for Paris in the morning. As an air mail pilot, he had learned to start out — and then turn back if he had to.

He got to bed around midnight. He couldn't sleep.

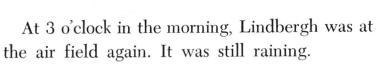

At 3 o'clock in the morning, Lindbergh was at the air field again. It was still raining.

He knew he couldn't take off from Curtiss Field. He would need a longer runway when the plane was carrying a full load of gasoline.

So, in the rainy darkness, a truck dragged the *Spirit of St. Louis* to Roosevelt Field, about a mile away.

Two men poured gas into the tanks, five gallons at a time. At last the tanks held 450 gallons — almost a ton and a half — of gas.

The pilots and crews of the other planes were there to say good-bye. No one knew if they would ever see Charles Lindbergh again.

It was after 7 o'clock in the morning when Lindbergh climbed into the cockpit.

The runway was muddy. Could he go fast enough in the mud to take off?

Was the plane too heavy? Lindbergh had never taken it up with a full load of gas.

He started the engine. What was the matter with the engine? It was turning over too slowly. Maybe the weather was slowing it down.

Maybe he shouldn't try to take off today. He had to decide now.

He buckled the safety belt and pulled his goggles over his eyes. He nodded to two men near the plane.

"Let's try it," he said.

The two men pulled the blocks out from under the wheels, and the *Spirit of St. Louis* moved slowly down the muddy runway.

Halfway down the runway, the plane made a little hop into the air. It was not moving fast enough to fly. A moment later it bounced back to the ground.

Another hop. Then another. The plane was going faster. Lindbergh was near the end of the runway now. One last try! This time the plane climbed a few feet into the air.

Lindbergh barely missed a tractor standing just beyond the runway. The plane climbed higher. Now Lindbergh was above the telephone wires.

He was on his way to Paris!

For the next day and a half, Lindbergh would
be sitting right where he was now. He couldn't
lie down, and he couldn't stand up.

The cockpit was so small, he could touch both
sides with his elbows. His head was less than an
inch from the roof.

The whole airplane was not even as long as a bus. It had a window on each side and one on top. It did not have a window in front. When Lindbergh wanted to see what was ahead of him, he had to use a home-made periscope.

There was no toilet on the plane, but there was a metal can with a lid.

Lindbergh had a bottle of water to drink, and five sandwiches to eat on the way — two ham sandwiches, two beef sandwiches, and a hard-boiled-egg sandwich.

"Are you only taking five sandwiches?" a friend had asked.

"I won't need more sandwiches if I get to Paris," Lindbergh answered. "And if I don't get to Paris, I won't need more either."

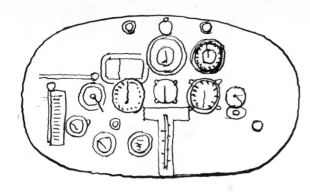

Instrument board of the *Spirit of St. Louis*

Besides, Lindbergh could get to Paris if he ran out of food. He knew he'd never get there if he ran out of gas. He wanted to have plenty of gas.

Gas was heavy. Every gallon weighed six pounds. So everything else on the plane had to be very light.

Lindbergh cut holes in his maps and charts so they would be lighter. He tore empty pages out of his notebook. He wasn't taking any extra clothes to wear in Paris. He did not even take a toothbrush.

He weighed every single thing he took with him. He took a rubber life raft in case he had to land at sea. But he didn't take a parachute, because a parachute weighed 20 pounds.

He had two small pocket flashlights instead of regular lights in the cockpit.

Lindbergh did not even have a radio. How would he be sure he was heading the right way? He had a compass. And before he left, he figured out his course and marked it on a chart. He would find Paris by following the chart.

By lunchtime, Lindbergh began getting tired and sleepy. The sun was shining into the cockpit, and he felt hot. His legs were stiff.

He had a drink of water, but he didn't feel like eating anything. He just wanted to go to sleep.

There were dark clouds ahead — storm clouds. "Stay awake!" he said to himself. "Stay awake!"

The clouds grew bigger and darker. Rain poured down. Lightning flashed. Lindbergh bumped up, down, and sideways in the cockpit. He was sorry he didn't have a parachute.

Soon the storm was over, but not for long. There were more clouds ahead. Lindbergh flew above the clouds, below them, between them.

Sometimes he had to fly right through the clouds. And sometimes he had to fly through fog, blinding white fog.

He got sleepier and more tired.

He stamped his feet. He sang a song out loud — very loud.

Lindbergh had been flying for 13 hours. It was dark now. The plane was shaking and bumping again. And the air was cold. Lindbergh zipped up his flying suit and put on his leather mittens and wool-lined helmet.

He pulled his flashlight from his pocket and let the light shine on the wings. Ice!

Ice on the wings! He could crash in this icy storm!

He thought of turning back.

Lindbergh's eyes kept closing. He had to hold them open with his fingers. He had been flying for 27 hours now.

Suddenly he saw a speck on the water. It was a boat! No, it was more than one boat. Those specks were fishing boats! Fishing boats couldn't be far from land. Was he near Ireland?

Lindbergh was wide awake now. He flew lower, close to the boats. A man stuck his head out of a porthole and looked up at him.

"Which way is Ireland?" Lindbergh yelled.

The man didn't move. Lindbergh thought that maybe the man was too surprised or too scared to answer.

Lindbergh flew on. In less than an hour he was over the rocky tip of Ireland. He saw green fields, roads, wagons, a little village. People ran into the streets and waved up at him.

In the late afternoon, Lindbergh flew over the coast of England.

He came to France just as it was getting dark. He had not eaten for almost two days. Now he ate one sandwich and drank some water.

And then he was flying over the Paris airport. He saw thousands of lights shining below him. They were the lights of automobiles. Thousands of people had come to welcome him and to light his way.

Charles Lindbergh landed in Paris on the night of May 21, 1927. He had been flying alone for 33½ hours. He had flown from New York to Paris without stopping, something no one had ever done before.

A few more facts
to go with some of the pages in this book

pages 4–5: You can visit the house and farm where Lindbergh grew up. They are in the Charles A. Lindbergh State Park near Little Falls, Minnesota.

pages 9 and 14–15: Lindbergh's first airplane was a Curtiss Jenny. It was a single-engine biplane — a plane with one engine and two sets of wings. The fastest a Jenny could go was 75 miles an hour, about as fast as a speeding car.

page 19: Two pilots, John Alcock and Arthur Brown, flew nonstop across the Atlantic Ocean in 1919 — but they flew from Newfoundland to Ireland, a distance of only about 1900 miles.

page 21: A monoplane is an airplane with one set of wings. When Lindbergh was deciding on his plane, monoplanes were new.

Why did Lindbergh want a plane with only one engine? Wouldn't it be safer to have three engines? No, said Lindbergh. There would be three times as many chances of having an engine quit.

Besides, Lindbergh said, a three-engine plane was big and heavy — harder to fly in bad weather. And another pilot would be needed to help fly a plane like that.

page 23: The company that made the plane was Ryan Airlines. You can see their name on the tail of the plane. NYP stands for *New York to Paris*, and NX–211 is the plane's license number — N for a United States plane that flies outside the country, and X for *experimental*.

pages 22, 24, and 27: How many other pilots were planning to fly across the Atlantic? The number of pilots — and planes — kept changing all the time.

Three or four French planes were supposed to fly from Paris to New York, but only one plane took off — and it was never seen again. In the United States, two planes crashed during test flights, and one crashed on take-off.

Lindbergh was 25 years old — the youngest of all the pilots who hoped to fly nonstop across the Atlantic Ocean.

page 25: Some of Lindbergh's other nicknames were Lindy, Lucky Lindy, the Flying Kid, the Lone Eagle, Silent Slim, and Slim. Except for Slim, he hated them all.

Lindbergh had always liked being alone, and that was one reason he wanted to fly across the ocean alone. He also wanted to make all the decisions himself. And he could take more gas if he flew alone. "I'd rather have extra gasoline than an extra man," he said.

page 34: Lindbergh was 6 feet 3 inches tall. He weighed 170 pounds.

page 35: The *Spirit of St. Louis* was 27 feet 8 inches long.

page 37: Some of the other things Lindbergh took with him in case he had to land in the water: 4 red flares (so passing ships could see him), 1 ball of string, 1 hunting knife, some extra water, and 5 cans of dry Army food.

Lindbergh opened one can of the Army food before he left. It tasted awful. "You'd have to be pretty hungry to eat the stuff," he said.

pages 44–45: For weeks after Lindbergh landed in Paris, there were parades, banquets, and celebrations for him. He was a hero.

Lindbergh wanted to fly the *Spirit of St. Louis* back to America. But the President of the United States sent a ship to France to bring Lindbergh and his plane home.

In Washington, D.C., and in New York, there were more parades — and then Lindbergh flew the *Spirit of St. Louis* on a good-will visit to every state in the United States and to Canada, Mexico, and South America.

Afterwards, Lindbergh gave the *Spirit of St. Louis* to the Smithsonian Institution in Washington, D.C., where you can see it now.

Lindbergh wrote two books about his famous flight — *"We,"* and *The Spirit of St. Louis.*

Some important dates in Charles Lindbergh's life

1902   Born in his grandparents' house in Detroit, Michigan, on February 4. Six weeks later, his mother brings him home to the family farm near Little Falls, Minnesota.

1920   Enters the University of Wisconsin to study engineering.

1922   Leaves college and takes eight flying lessons. Barnstorms, makes his first parachute jump, and is nicknamed Daredevil Lindbergh.

1923   Buys his first airplane, a Jenny, and makes his first solo flight.

1924–25   Learns more about flying as an Army flying cadet, then goes back to barnstorming.

1926   In April, gets job as an airmail pilot. In September, decides to fly nonstop across the Atlantic Ocean by himself.

1927   On May 20, Lindbergh takes off from Roosevelt Field and is the first person to fly nonstop from New York City to Paris, France.

1929   Marries Anne Morrow on May 27. Between 1930 and 1945, the Lindberghs have six children — four boys and two girls. Their first child, a son, is kidnapped and murdered in 1932.

1931   With Anne Morrow Lindbergh as his radio operator, Lindbergh flies a single-engine monoplane to China. This flight and many others are made to plan routes for new airlines.

1941–44   Serves as a consultant to companies that make planes for World War II, and later flies as a combat pilot in the Pacific.

1946–74   Is a consultant to Pan American World Airways and to the U.S. Government, but becomes more and more interested in wildlife conservation and the environment.

1974   Lindbergh learns he is about to die of cancer and asks to be flown to his little house on the island of Maui, Hawaii. He dies there on August 26 at the age of 72.